MENSTRUATION

menstruation

A FIRST BOOK
REVISED EDITION
BY ALAN E.
NOURSE, M.D.

FRANKLIN WATTS   NEW YORK   LONDON   TORONTO   SYDNEY   1987

DIAGRAMS BY ANNE CANEVARI GREEN

Library of Congress Cataloging-in-Publication Data

Nourse, Alan Edward.
Menstruation.

(A First book)
Rev. ed. of: Menstruation, just plain talk. 1980.
Includes index.
Summary: Discusses the menstrual cycle,
abnormalities and their treatment, and the
significance of menstruation in one's life.
Includes a glossary of medical terms.
1. Menstruation—Juvenile literature.
2. Menstruation disorders—Juvenile literature.
[1. Menstruation] I. Nourse, Alan Edward.
Menstruation, just plain talk. II. Title.
RG161.N59 1987   612′.662   86-24732
ISBN 0-531-10308-0

CONTENTS

FOREWORD

The first menstrual period has always been a very important event in the life of the adolescent girl. In the days of our grand-mothers and great-grandmothers, little was known about how a woman's body functioned; consequently, there were many myths and misconceptions surrounding this event. Very often the happiness and pride which should be evident upon reaching this milestone on the path toward becoming an adult were distorted by the secrecy surrounding menstruation and the fear caused by insufficient knowledge of normal bodily processes. Many girls quickly learned that most adults, including moth-ers and doctors, felt very uncomfortable discussing menstrua-tion. Their questions went unasked and unanswered. Often this secrecy was perpetuated because of the unproven belief that by informing teenagers about their developing bodies, one might somehow encourage sexual experimentation.

We now know that information is not as dangerous as ignorance. The more we know and understand about how our bodies work, the easier it is to care for them wisely and well. Today, people of all ages are much healthier and live longer than in grandmother's day. This fortunate state of affairs is partially due to the vast increase in medical knowledge that has occurred during this century. We have every reason to believe that as women become more informed and less ashamed of the complex and wonderful workings of their bodies, they will become healthier in all aspects of their lives, both physically and emotionally.

However, gaining information about her body and her feelings is not an easy task for the young adolescent. She must gain this information at a time when she is trying to achieve some independence from her parents as well as from other adults. This normal and very necessary process of separation from family, which begins in early adolescence, places a strain upon the usual lines of communication between parent and child. Parents must learn to convey information in a manner which allows these emerging adults to make some of their own decisions. Similarly, teenagers must somehow learn just when they are truly capable of making intelligent judgments and when they are still in need of informed adult advice. This delicate balance is even more precarious when the issues to be learned and discussed deal with developing sexuality. Often their own fears and lack of information lead parents to avoid discussion of this sensitive area. Further, a developing sense of privacy and embarrassment regarding sexual issues may steer the teenager away from the support of even the most understanding parents.

Menstruation has a significant role to play in this common family situation. It allows the teenage girl to inform herself and find answers to her questions about her body and menstruation in a private and independent way. It encourages her to accept responsibility for understanding how her body functions and how to care for it. The book provides an excellent introduction to the fascinating workings of the female body. There is a clear, accurate description of the normal processes of adolescence including an explanation of the events occurring during a menstrual cycle. Both common normal variations and abnormal situations are discussed in a way that will help the teenager decide which occurrences might require medical attention. Current approaches to treatment of abnormal situations are outlined in a manner that allows for easy understanding by the younger reader.

One of the most helpful aspects of this book is that it emphasizes the proper vocabulary for describing puberty and menstruation. We are told the names of the important glands, organs, and hormones and are even given the historical derivation of some of these words. As a first step toward understanding any new subject, the vocabulary is essential. After reading this book, teenagers will be able to ask their questions and discuss their concerns with much more confidence and accuracy.

I would highly recommend this book to all young teenagers and their parents. The information presented is simple, clear and up-to-date. When read by parent and child this book will serve not as a substitute for discussion but rather as a stimulus to the exchange of information and feelings between parent and adolescent.

Susan Coupey, M.D.
Division of Adolescent Medicine
Montefiore Hospital
and Medical Center
Bronx, New York

WHAT'S GOING ON? | 1

For virtually every girl reading this book, there will come a day in her early teenage years when she reaches a major turning point in her physical life, the day she first begins menstruating.

What exactly is **menstruation**? In plainest possible terms, it is a flow of blood and cell fragments that passes from the interior of the **uterus**, or womb, down the **vagina** to the outside of the body at more or less regular intervals. Menstrual periods, or just plain **periods**, usually begin in the early teenage years and continue until a woman is about forty-five or fifty years old. The word **menstruation** actually comes from the Latin word *mensa,* meaning "month," since the average interval from the start of one menstrual period to the start of the next is about twenty-eight days, roughly a month according to the ancient Roman calendar. Doctors call the flow itself **menses**. It usually lasts from four to six days, a little less for some, a little more for others. A girl's very first menstrual period is called her **menarche** (pronounced men-AR-key). The girl's periods will not normally be suspended, then, except during pregnancies, until she reaches **menopause**, or "end of menstruation," many years later.

No one can say when your menstrual periods will begin. For some of you, they will already have started; for others not yet. Menarche is determined to some extent by heredity. In addition, certain physical signs, such as breast enlargement and the appearance of body hair in places where it wasn't previously, usually precede the onset of menstruation by about one and a half to two and a half years. But no matter when your menstruation does begin, it is an outward and obvious sign that some very striking changes are going on inside your physically maturing body.

Menstruation may appear suddenly, but it is not something that just suddenly happens, like a snap of the fingers or a blink of the eye. Rather, it is the last in a long series of chemical and biological events, events that begin months or even years before the first menstruation occurs. Starting to menstruate is an important sign of **puberty**, that time of life during which a person's mature sexual self emerges. But it is only one such sign.

Perhaps you have already read some things about menstruation. Maybe you have attended a health or hygiene course or seen a movie at school. Certainly many of you will have talked to your mothers, older sisters, or friends about the subject. But chances are that the whole business of menstruation is still somewhat unclear, puzzling, maybe even frightening to many of you. What's going on here? Why menstruation, of all things?

There is usually no need for apprehension about menstruation. Yet sometimes seemingly odd or different things do happen, and when they do, questions arise.

FOUR GIRLS

Let's consider the very different things that happened to four girls, whose names have been changed but whose stories are based on actual experiences.

• To her mother's considerable distress, Janie McC. began her first menstrual period just three weeks after her ninth birthday. Both she and her mother had noticed a significant amount of breast enlargement for some months before the menstrual period occurred. This sign of sexual maturity had already upset Janie's mother, who felt it was appearing unusually early. But when Janie's menstruation began before she was even ten years old, her mother promptly took her to a doctor. What was going on here?

• Karen K.'s story was quite different. Karen had her first menstrual period just before her thirteenth birthday—exactly when you might have expected it to occur—but then she didn't have another period for eight solid months. When it finally did come, her second period was so very scant that it hardly seemed like a period at all. Then again, months passed without any further menstruation. Finally, convinced that something was terribly wrong, Karen's mother took her to see the doctor. What was going on?

• At least Karen K. did have a menstrual period at about the time in her life when it was expected. Pamela C. did not. Although other signs of sexual maturity began appearing when she was thirteen or fourteen years old, Pamela still had not had a menstrual period of any sort by the time she was sixteen. She seemed perfectly well and happy, and she objected to being bothered with a visit to the doctor, but her mother insisted. What was going on?

• Sherry D.'s earliest menstrual experiences raised a different kind of question. Her first period, at age twelve, seemed perfectly normal—but with each of her next three periods she complained of such severe cramps that she couldn't go to school for three days each time. Her mother (who had never had cramps with her periods) was suspicious. She knew Sherry was upset about menstruating—she hadn't been prepared, and her first period took her by surprise. Were the "cramps" she complained of just in her mind, or was she really having pain for some reason? Again, a trip to the doctor seemed indicated. What was really going on here?

In fact, nothing terribly unusual was going on with any one of these four girls. True enough, Janie's sexual maturity and the beginning of her menstrual periods came surprisingly early. But, as her doctor explained, it was still at the early edge of the normal age range when these events can occur. While *most* girls begin their periods somewhere between age eleven and age fourteen, there are a few who start earlier and a few who start later. Of course Janie's doctor took a careful medical history, looking for any sign of possible trouble, and performed a thorough physical examination. In addition, he collected a blood sample to be tested for certain chemical or hormonal imbalances, to be as sure as he could that Janie was not suffering from some rare disorder of growth and development. But, as he expected, nothing abnormal was found. Janie McC. was in the peak of good health, had nothing wrong with her, and was simply one of 3 or 4 percent of all girls who begin menstruating very early.

Normal good health was the doctor's verdict for Karen K. as well. After performing a simple physical exam to assure himself of this fact, the doctor explained to Karen and her mother that while many girls who begin menstruating at the age of thirteen or so proceed to have an orderly and regular schedule of menstrual periods right from the start, many others do not. Indeed, the doctor said, it was perfectly normal for a girl to have as much as a year or two of irregular periods before a regular pattern became established. The doctor said that he would not advise any treatment at this time. He added that if Karen's irregular periods continued beyond what he considered normal, treatment was available and might at that time be advisable. In this case, however, treatment did not prove necessary. Karen had a third and normal menstrual period soon after her visit to the doctor and had a fourth a month later. Her periods remained somewhat unpredictable and irregular for another year, but they gradually settled down to a reliable twenty-six-day interval and remained that way from then on.

Pamela C.'s situation seemed a bit more mysterious to her doctor until he learned one vital fact about her life: Pamela, it turned out, was an extraordinarily active young woman. She was, in fact, deeply involved in gymnastics, one of the most brutally demanding and strenuous of all athletic activities. Pamela had been attending a special gymnastics school and was being privately coached as well in hopes of someday becoming an Olympics contender. She was spending as much as six to eight hours a day in the gymnasium, day after day, developing her strength, timing, precision, and physical control.

The doctor pointed out that this excessive activity might well be delaying Pamela's menstruation. Scientific studies, he said, had shown that girls who are engaged in extreme physical activity over prolonged periods often begin menstruating later than other girls—or may stop menstruating if they have already begun. Of course, the doctor said, these girls do catch up sooner or later. Very often when they take a lengthy vacation from their physical activity or catch a bad case of flu and have to rest for a while, they suddenly begin menstruating.

As for Sherry D.'s problem—cramping with her menstrual periods—the doctor that Sherry saw was particularly sympathetic because she, too, had had trouble with menstrual cramping as a younger woman. She explained to Sherry and her mother that a great many girls had some degree of menstrual cramping at one time or another, sometimes quite regularly. With most such people, the doctor said, it was a real physical problem, not just "mental." And although it wasn't exactly *normal*, it wasn't necessarily a cause for alarm, either, because things could be done about it. In many cases, the doctor said, just taking a simple **analgesic** or pain medication such as aspirin or Tylenol for a couple of days during the period would do the trick; if not, other measures would be effective. (We will have more to say about the causes and treatment of menstrual cramping a bit later.)

FANTASIES AND FAIRY TALES

Clearly menstruation can vary a great deal from one person to another and still fall within normal range. Equally clearly, menstruation is a normal bodily function of girls who are maturing sexually. You might think that anything so normal and so commonplace—after all, half the people in the world have periodic menstruation throughout a large part of their lives—would simply be accepted by everyone as okay, natural, even rather nice; a sign that things are going the way they are supposed to.

Actually, attitudes toward menstruation could not be more opposite. Until very recently, any mention of menstruation was considered thoroughly taboo—forbidden—except in very private and embarrassed circumstances. In fact, throughout most of history, menstruation has been regarded with apprehension, shame, embarrassment, and distress. It has been the cause of innumerable social rules that have restricted the lives and activities of young women everywhere, and the subject of all sorts of ridiculous folk tales, beliefs, and scare stories, virtually all of them untrue. What is more, many of these restrictive rules, practices, and foolish stories remain active even today.

You may already have noticed, for example, that almost nobody refers to menstruation by its actual name. Any number of other words are used instead. Often you will hear it called "the curse," based upon the idea that it is a sort of woman's burden. Other times you may hear it called "the friend," perhaps referring to the fact that the beginning of a menstrual flow is a sign that a woman is not pregnant, and thus the period's appearance is greeted with relief by a woman who has been worried about this. Some girls have their own private names that they use based on purely personal experience. Other terms, such as "falling off the roof" or "falling out of bed," defy explanation.

Just as there are many names for menstruation that suggest it is something shameful or disgusting, there are any number of strange and curious beliefs about this natural bodily function that suggest there is something wrong with a woman who is menstruating. Even today there are people who believe that a menstruating woman would cause milk to sour, wine to turn to vinegar, the leaves of houseplants to droop, or cut flowers to wilt. Innumerable girls believe that they smell bad during menstruation, which is totally untrue as long as they pay normal attention to their physical cleanliness. Others mistakenly believe that to miss a period means serious physical harm because it keeps in bad blood that needs to come out. Girls beyond number have been carefully taught that to go swimming during a menstrual period is practically sudden death and that physical activity during a period should be severely restricted. Some girls really believe that the only thing to do during a period is to go to bed with a cold towel on their foreheads.

Even worse, a number of girls approaching their first period are secretly terrified by stories they have heard about extreme blood loss, agonizing pain, or some sort of terrible physical impairment. Far more come to think of menstruation as a *mal*function of their bodies, something that is shameful and too awful to think about. Still other girls have been told that to menstruate means you are a woman, and they are frightened because they don't understand what this involves.

Many of the negative attitudes and feelings that put down or degrade menstruation have their roots in cultures or religions thousands of years old. Two hundred years ago, long before disposable pads or tampons were thought of to control menses in a convenient and sanitary manner, women in parts of Italy were being taught that to even mention they were menstruating was wrong. These women used cloths to absorb their flow, and they had to hide the cloths in cracks in the wall until they could later secretly wash them out for reuse. Many societies associated pain, distress, and disgust with menstruation. Some primitive tribes forced women to remain alone in their huts during menstrual periods. Natives of the Aleutian islands would not allow a menstruating female near the water, for fear that she would spoil the fishing.

In ancient Hebrew societies, a woman was regarded as sexually "unclean" during her period plus an extra seven days after her flow had stopped. During that time she and her husband were not permitted to have sexual relations nor to sleep in the same bed. They were not even supposed to touch each other. At the end of the seven days, the woman would immerse herself in a river or lake or special indoor pool as a purification ritual.

Society's restrictive rules disappear very slowly. And considering the many strange beliefs, stories, and myths that have grown up around menstruation, it is hardly any wonder that so many girls are still in the dark as to what is *really* going on. Why does menstruation occur in the first place? What is true about it and what is not? To find clear, understandable answers we first need some basic facts about the events that occur in a girl's body as she approaches sexual maturity—events that ultimately lead to menstruation.

JUST THE FACTS, MA'AM

2

As we said earlier, menstruation is not something that just suddenly happens. It is the last in a long series of chemical and biological events, and every one of those events depends upon the action of chemical substances in the body called **hormones.** Thus, before we can understand what menstruation is all about, we must first know something about what these hormones do.

PREPARING FOR REPRODUCTION

Actually, menstruation is just one rather minor part of a much larger bodily function known as the **female reproductive cycle,** every part of which is controlled from the start by the action of certain hormones.

All hormones are powerful chemical substances. Many of them are produced in the body in special organs called **glands**; others are produced by cells in special areas such as the brain or the lining of the uterus. Sometimes we speak of hormones as chemical messengers, or chemicals that act at a distance. This

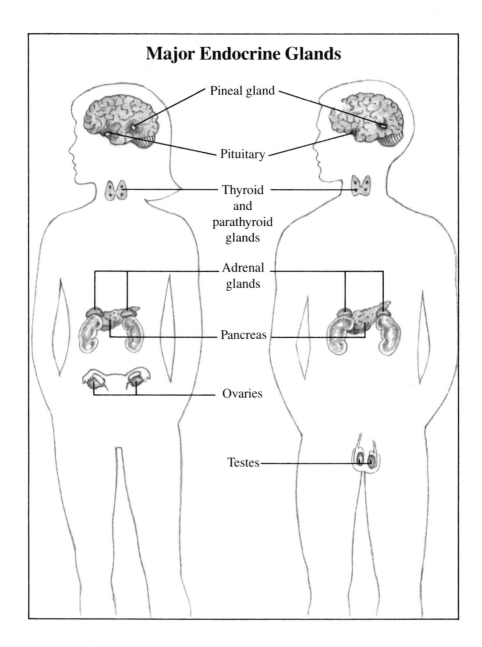

Major Endocrine Glands

Pineal gland

Pituitary

Thyroid
and
parathyroid
glands

Adrenal
glands

Pancreas

Ovaries

Testes

is because most hormones (including many that are concerned with reproduction) are produced in glands in one part of the body and then travel by way of the bloodstream to other, distant organs to bring about their effect. However, some of the most important hormones involved in human reproduction are produced in the so-called **sex glands**, which in the female are the **ovaries** and in the male are the **testicles.** Still other reproductive hormones are produced in the outer shell, or *cortex,* of the **adrenal glands,** which sit perched like little caps on top of the kidneys. Finally, some very important reproductive hormones are formed in the **pituitary gland**, a tiny gland that lies deep inside the skull at the base of the brain, or in an area of the brain called the **hypothalamus** which lies in direct contact with the pituitary gland.

Oddly enough, the first effects of these reproductive hormones that we actually see don't really have very much to do with reproduction at all—at least not directly. Just as the soil in a garden must be prepared before vegetables can grow in it, the body must be prepared before it can ultimately become capable of reproduction. The first reproductive hormone activities that we see are, in a sense, preparing the ground for things that will happen later.

Consider first what happens to a girl as she approaches her eleventh or twelfth birthday. Most girls at the age of nine or ten closely resemble boys of the same age in physical size and shape. They tend to be thin, flat-chested, and gangly. They are all bones and angles. Their bodies are largely hairless except for the hair on their heads, and their voices have just about the same high pitch as the boys. Many girls in this age group engage and compete in the same games as boys, and play—or fight—with boys on pretty even ground.

Sooner or later, however, certain differences begin to

appear. At about age eleven or twelve, sometimes a little earlier, sometimes a little later, a girl undergoes a sudden surge of physical growth. She becomes taller. Her bones become longer and heavier, and she develops larger and stronger muscles than before. In some girls this so-called **growth spurt** is so quiet and subtle that it is hardly even noticed; in others it may be quite marked. In either case, the end of this period of growth will determine how tall and heavy-boned the girl will be throughout the rest of her life.

During the growth spurt, signs of sexual maturity are also beginning to appear. The girl's breasts begin to enlarge and will continue to develop for a period of two to three years. Pubic hair begins to appear between the legs. Hair also starts to grow under the arms. The girl will develop a layer of fat on the shoulders and hips that will change her "string bean" appearance to a more rounded and curvy shape. Although her voice will not change dramatically, it will usually become more mature and less babyish than it was before. And along with all these changes, her uterus will be developing to adult size and her external genital organs will become more mature. Finally, the girl may find herself becoming more interested in boys as *boys* rather than just as competitors on the baseball field.

THE SECONDARY
SEX CHARACTERISTICS

All these changes are primarily the work of certain female sex hormones that have begun to be produced in the girl's ovaries. The most important of these hormones are called **estrogens**, meaning, literally, "estrus makers," a term that applies to periods of special sexual readiness or "heat" common to female dogs, cats, and other lower animals. Human females have no such special intervals reserved for sexual activity, but the term seems to have stuck.

Doctors speak of these physical changes as **secondary sex characteristics** because none of them is directly involved with reproduction at all—at first. Yet they do prepare the girl's body for a future pregnancy in some important ways.

Of course boys, too, develop secondary sex characteristics. The growth spurt in boys, usually occurring between ages twelve and fifteen, may be very striking, with as much as a foot (30 cm) or more in height gained in a matter of a year or two. The boy's bones become longer and heavier than the girl's, his muscles more massive. He, too, develops underarm and pubic hair and his sexual organs become larger and more mature. (He will also start to grow a rudimentary beard and moustache, although this may be delayed for several years.) Because of a sudden enlargement in his larynx, or voice box, a boy's voice will drop to a lower register after an awkward period of adjustment. At this point he, too, will be physically prepared for his mature reproductive functions as a male.

The hormones that produce these male secondary sex characteristics are the so-called male sex hormones, or **androgens**, from Greek words meaning "man maker." They are primarily produced in the testicles, although some are also produced in the adrenal glands. Actually, these so-called male and female sex hormones are by no means exclusively restricted to males and females respectively, as one might think. Although boys have a preponderance of androgens, their bodies also produce some estrogens. And while girls have predominantly estrogens, their bodies also produce small amounts of androgens. One proof of this fact is that many teenage girls suffer from that hated adolescent plague known as **acne**, or pimples, just as severely as boys do. But we know that the skin changes of ado-

lescent acne are, in large part, a result of increased *androgen* activity in the body. A girl doesn't have to have very much androgen to stimulate acne; a little bit is all it takes. But if she had no androgens at all in her body, she would not develop acne.

THE OVULATION CYCLE

The secondary sex characteristics, in themselves, may not seem very important. They do result in girls beginning to look more like young women and boys more like young men. And they are proof positive that certain glands in the body are beginning to mature and produce male or female sex hormones in considerable quantity. They are a sign of approaching sexual maturity. But from nature's point of view, the whole idea of a girl or boy becoming sexually mature is to make it possible for reproduction to take place—for a new human being to be formed. This requires a special cell—an egg cell, or **ovum** (pl. **ova**)—to be ripened and released in one of the girl's ovaries. The ovum carries half the hereditary information needed to create a new baby. Reproduction also requires the production of a special **sperm** cell in the young man's testicles—again a cell carrying half the hereditary information necessary to generate a new human baby. Boys begin to manufacture sperm during puberty and continue to do so for most of their lives. The special male and female reproductive cells—sometimes called **germ cells**—normally meet as a result of sexual relations. In order for a pregnancy to occur, they must fuse together, or unite, in a process known as **fertilization.**

Sperm can be produced by the millions at almost any time, but nature is far more sparing in the production of mature or *ripened* ova. Ordinarily, mature ova are produced just one at a

time, each one carefully prepared and released in the girl's body under the direction of special hormones. (On rare occasions, two ova may mature and be fertilized at the same time, leading to a twin pregnancy with nonidentical or "fraternal" twins.) One could think of the production of each individual ovum as a major attempt on nature's part to make reproduction possible. If one attempt fails, nature makes another attempt, and then another and another in a recurring, repeated cycle that, once started, continues for some forty years.

From the time of birth on, a girl's ovaries contain a lifetime supply of tiny, immature ova, just lying at rest—as many as four hundred thousand of them, according to some experts! Each one of these immature ova is surrounded by a cluster or nest of protective cells. These microscopic nests are known as **follicles**, from the Latin word meaning "pod" or "shell." For the first ten years or so of a girl's life, none of these follicles changes much. Then at puberty, ranging from around age eleven to age thirteen, a special hormone is produced in the girl's pituitary gland and is released in tiny quantities into her bloodstream, where it travels to her ovaries. This special hormone is the **follicle-stimulating hormone** or **FSH.**

As you might guess from the name, the job of FSH is to stimulate the growth of cells in one single follicle, so that the ovum at that follicle's center will begin to enlarge and mature. But one hormone is not enough. After seven or eight days a second hormone from the pituitary gland appears and triggers the final enlargement and ripening of the ovum. Eventually the mature ovum breaks free from the follicle and is caught in the upper end of the **Fallopian tube** which is wrapped around the ovary. From there it is conducted slowly down into the upper end of the tube, where it can come in contact with a sperm cell and become fertilized. This process—the enlarge-

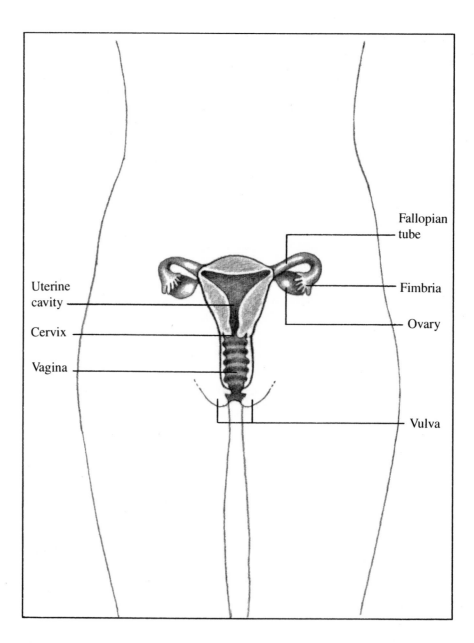

Fallopian tube

Fimbria

Ovary

Uterine cavity

Cervix

Vagina

Vulva

ment and release of a mature ovum into the Fallopian tube—is known as **ovulation**, and it is nature's grand attempt to make reproduction possible. As soon as the ovum is free from the follicle, that same second hormone that helped the process of ovulation earlier immediately begins acting on the follicle cells left behind, causing them to form a small lump of pinkish yellow tissue called the **corpus luteum** (from Latin words meaning "yellow body"). For that reason, this second hormone is called **luteinizing hormone, or LH.**

Of course this new mature ovum will need a safe place to grow and develop if it becomes fertilized by a sperm. Again, it is hormones that set the stage. It takes about eight to ten days from the earliest sign of ripening of an immature ovum in a follicle to the time the mature ovum is released. During that time, estrogens from the ovaries are very busy acting on cells lining the inside of the woman's uterus. The estrogens cause those cells to multiply, or *proliferate*, very fast and to form special tiny blood vessels and tiny nurturing glands as they grow. By the time ovulation occurs, the uterine lining has become quite thick, with a rich blood supply. What is more, just after the ovum is released, that pinkish yellow lump of tissue left behind in the ovary begins to produce a completely different hormone. Its job is to act on that enlarged lining of the uterus to make it soft and spongy and to make the glands in it begin to secrete sugars and other nutrients. This hormone is called **progesterone**, from Latin words meaning "ahead of pregnancy."

Last of all, yet another hormone, this one also from the pituitary gland, keeps prodding the corpus luteum to produce more and more progesterone, thus making sure that there is plenty of this "pregnancy-protecting" hormone around at the right time. Because this new hormone at a later stage works in

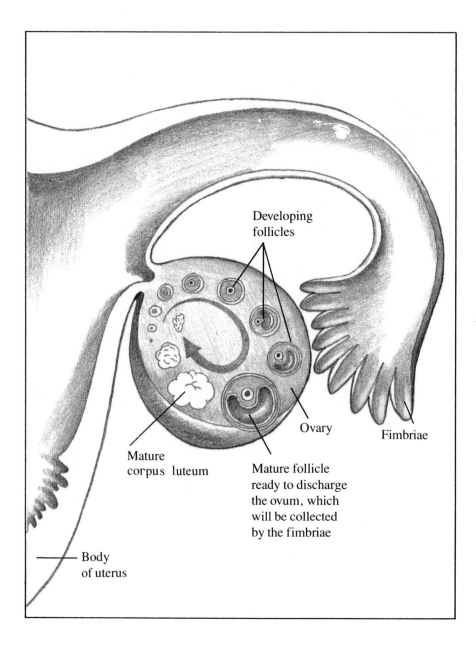

Developing follicles

Ovary

Fimbriae

Mature corpus luteum

Mature follicle ready to discharge the ovum, which will be collected by the fimbriae

Body of uterus

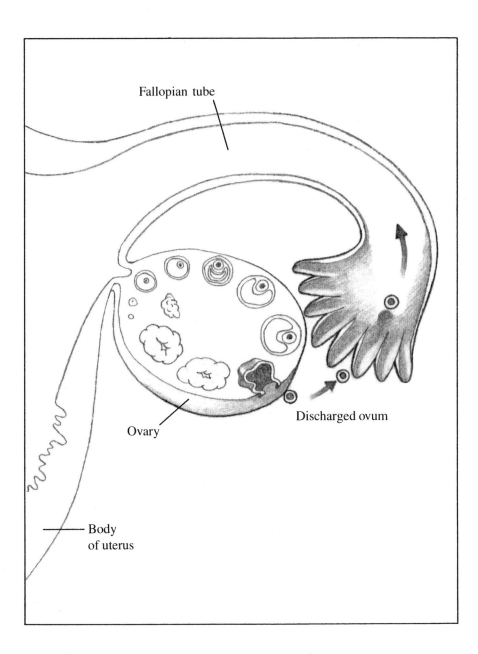

Fallopian tube

Ovary

Discharged ovum

Body
of uterus

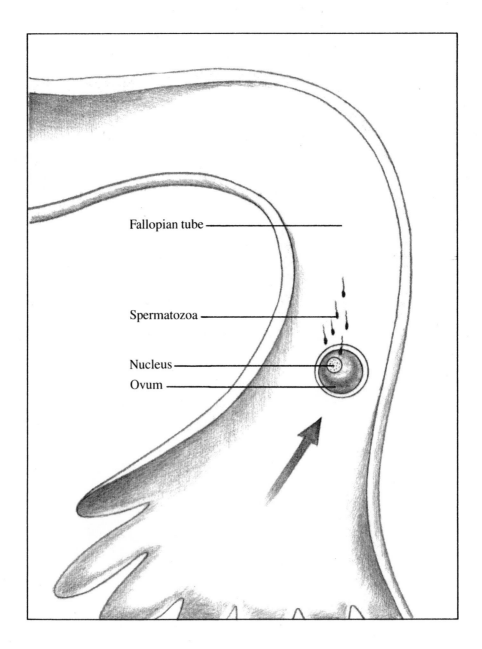

Fallopian tube

Spermatozoa

Nucleus

Ovum

partnership with estrogens to enlarge the woman's breasts and prepare them for milk production if she becomes pregnant, it is often called a **lactogenic,** "milk-producing," **hormone,** or simply **prolactin,** which means "before the milk."

All this may seem terribly complicated at first glance, but actually it makes perfect sense once you understand the point of it. The woman's body is making a grand attempt at reproduction, producing a mature ovum ready to be fertilized and, at the same time, preparing a safe place for it to lodge and grow into a baby should it become fertilized. In order to accomplish these things a whole series of events has taken place, each event directed by a special hormone. And, except for one or two possible happenings, there is no clue or signal to tell the woman that any of these hormone-directed activities is taking place. Once in a while, in some women, a bit of fluid may escape into the abdomen just when the ripened ovum breaks free from its follicle, and this fluid may cause some twinges of discomfort in the lower abdomen right at ovulation time. This discomfort, called **mittelschmerz,** a German word meaning "pain in the middle," can give the woman a clue that ovulation has taken place. But since it only happens to some women, and then only sometimes, it cannot be taken as a reliable sign of ovulation. More predictably, in most women the normal, resting body temperature will increase slightly—perhaps half a degree Fahrenheit—when ovulation takes place, and will remain slightly elevated for several days thereafter. The woman who is especially eager to know exactly when she ovulates in order to help her become pregnant (or avoid becoming pregnant) may be able to measure this "basal temperature change" when it occurs—but the average person might find it difficult to be sure without a great deal of experience in temperature taking.

ENTER MENSTRUATION

Obviously, up until ovulation, nothing is decided as far as nature's attempt at reproduction is concerned. It is during ovulation that the all-important step takes place. At that time a particular ovum can meet up with a sperm cell and become fertilized. But if it does not, the ovum will simply disintegrate within a matter of just forty-eight hours or so. The corpus luteum will begin to shrink and stop producing progesterone. Several days later the specially prepared lining of the uterus, with its glands and many small blood vessels, will begin to break down. A quantity of cellular material and a certain amount of blood will then pass down through the lower end of the uterus, known as the **cervix**, and be carried out of the body by way of the vagina in a typical menstrual period. Ordinarily the amount of menses, or menstrual flow, is not very great, usually no more than five or six tablespoonsful. Ordinarily the amount of blood that is lost is very sharply limited because natural body processes soon pinch off the vessels that have supplied the uterine lining with blood. This allows the lining of the uterus to return very quickly to its original state, which it will maintain until the next ripened ovum is released.

MENSTRUATION AND PREGNANCY

All in all, a menstrual period is simply the end point in the female body's attempt at reproduction. That a menstrual period occurs tells us that this one particular attempt failed. The ovum was not fertilized by a sperm, so no pregnancy occurred.

Of course, the body does not stop after just one attempt. Soon after the period is over, the levels of follicle-stimulating hormones from the pituitary gland once again rise in the wom-

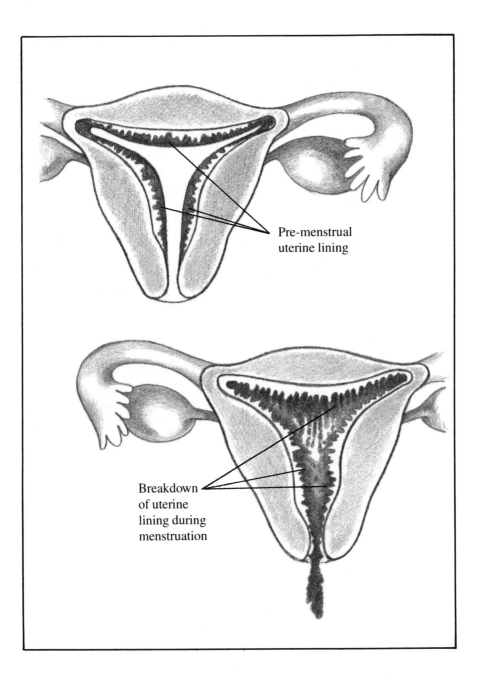

Pre-menstrual
uterine lining

Breakdown
of uterine
lining during
menstruation

an's bloodstream and start the development of another ovum. Estrogens again begin building up the inner lining of the uterus, the mature ovum is presently released into the Fallopian tube, and the whole ovulation cycle is carried out once more. If the woman never becomes pregnant, this cycle will be repeated at roughly twenty-eight-day intervals (the exact times will vary a few days from one woman to another) until she reaches her late forties or early fifties. At that point in her life—that is, at menopause—a woman's production of sex hormones diminishes, she no longer ovulates, and her menstrual periods come to an end.

The story would be totally different if the mature ovum happened to become fertilized by contact with a sperm. The fertilized ovum would then find its way down into the uterus and become embedded in the special lining of tissue that had been prepared there. Progesterone hormones would continue to be produced to help protect and maintain the pregnancy, and would soon stimulate formation of a special organ known as the **placenta** to nourish the growing **embryo.** Soon the placenta itself would begin producing still more progesterone to help protect the pregnancy throughout its term. Because this attempt at reproduction had succeeded, there would be no menstruation. Instead, other hormone-induced signs of pregnancy would begin to appear—breast enlargement, for example, or episodes of nausea. What is more, the progesterone hormones would also work to block the development of any new ova until the pregnancy is over, since the woman's body is normally only able to take care of one pregnancy at a time. The woman would not ordinarily begin ovulating again until at least two or three months after the baby was finally delivered, perhaps even longer. And the first evidence that she *was* ovulating again would be the appearance of the first normal menstrual period after her pregnancy was over.

Many women have the idea that since menstruation is so closely related to pregnancy, they can use their menstrual periods alone to tell when they are most likely to become pregnant. Unfortunately, this just doesn't work. It would be more accurate to say that menstruation is closely related to *non*pregnancy. Appearance of the menstrual period is usually good evidence that a pregnancy has *not* occurred during the last ovulation cycle. If it had, there wouldn't be any menstrual period. But a normal period tells you nothing whatever about when your body will produce and release its *next* mature ovum. There is no set interval of time between the beginning of a menstrual period and the time of the next ovulation.

Indeed, the only thing that is at all reliable is the amount of time between ovulation and the beginning of the menstrual period that follows—if fertilization hasn't taken place. This is usually about ten days and, within a day or so, applies to most women. Thus, when your period begins, you can look back and say, "Gee, about ten days ago I must have ovulated." But there is no way to pinpoint that critical ovulation day ahead of time based on menstrual periods alone.

Perhaps the most important thing to recognize about menstruation is that it is a perfectly normal, logical, and sensible stage in a reproductive cycle that repeats itself over and over again, usually interrupted only when a pregnancy occurs. Fortunately, under ordinary circumstances, normal body activities work smoothly and neatly. You rarely see abnormalities appearing. Of course, because you are an individual, your pattern of menstruation will be an individual thing. But the *range of normalcy* can be very broad.

Now that we have seen what menstruation is and why it occurs, we need to consider some of the individual variations that girls may encounter and see what, if anything, they may mean.

WHAT'S NORMAL AND WHAT'S NOT?

3

Even though menstruation is a normal bodily function, its physical effects can vary a great deal from one person to another. What is more, some girls do indeed experience definite and distressing *ab*normalities with their periods, and almost certainly each one of you will, sooner or later, hear stories about abnormalities that others have experienced. So how on earth can you tell what's normal and what's not?

When problems with menstruation do occur, they are not usually imaginary, or "all in a woman's head." They are very real problems arising for real physical reasons, and in most cases they can be successfully treated. The rest of this chapter should help you decide whether sensations and feelings you experience in relation to your menstruation are within the range of normal or whether they require a doctor's attention.

TOO EARLY OR TOO LATE

Everything would be much simpler if all girls began menstruating on their thirteenth birthday, but, as we have seen, they don't. There is a range of normal extending from about age ten through age fourteen. But what about those who begin even earlier or later than this range of normal? These girls are in "problem areas." In most cases nothing whatever is wrong: the girl is simply at the extreme end of the range of normal. But the girl who begins menstruating at age eight or nine, or one who has not menstruated by the time she is fifteen, could have a real physical problem and should have the benefit of a doctor's advice.

What kind of physical problems are we talking about? When they exist, they almost always involve either some kind of hormone disturbance in the body, or an anatomical abnormality of some sort—some peculiarity in the physical structure of the body. We have already seen that all the chemical events that trigger the ovulation cycle and keep it humming smoothly are brought about by the action of hormones produced primarily in the ovaries, the pituitary gland, or the adrenal glands. An abnormal growth in any of those glands could change the amount of one or another hormone released in the bloodstream and throw the pattern off. For example, a girl could develop a collection of fluid known as a **cyst** in one of her ovaries, which could disturb that gland's normal function and prevent it from producing the right amount of estrogen. On the other hand, the girl might develop a small **tumor**—an overgrowth of cells—in an ovary, which could cause the gland to produce excessive amounts of estrogen. Either way, the regularity of the ovulation cycle might be disturbed. Similarly, a tumor in the pituitary gland or in the cortex of the adrenal gland might also cause hormone excesses or hormone shortages.

Fortunately, modern medical techniques can pin down such problems quite rapidly. An ovarian cyst, for example, can often be detected during a simple physical examination. X rays or scanning techniques can help the doctor diagnose adrenal or pituitary gland abnormalities, and special laboratory studies of blood or urine known as hormone assays make it possible to tell which hormones, if any, are present in too large or too small a supply. Once the nature of the trouble has been diagnosed, any of these problems can be treated and, usually, cured.

Anatomical malformations—that is, abnormalities in body structure—can also be readily recognized. Perhaps the most common and simple-to-diagnose malformation is the so-called **imperforate hymen**. In this condition it is the thin sheet of tissue called the **hymen**, or maidenhead, that is causing the problem. Until sexual relations have begun, the hymen normally covers part of the opening to the vagina. But in the case of an imperforate hymen, the tissue may actually block the outlet severely or even completely, leaving little or no way for the menstrual flow to escape. A simple, painless operation in a doctor's office can remove a bit of tissue and solve the problem without further ado. In more complicated (and extremely rare) cases, a girl may be found to have a **double uterus**, a **double cervix**, or even a **double vagina**, all abnormalities that arose while her body was first developing inside her mother's womb. When such a rare situation is found, expert consultation will point the direction to the best possible treatment.

IRREGULAR OR UNPREDICTABLE MENSTRUATION

While some girls develop a perfectly regular pattern of periods from their first menstrual period on, many girls have quite irregular periods for the first six months, perhaps even for a year or two. Sometimes the periods may not only be unpredictable as to timing, but may vary a good deal from period to period in the amount and duration of flow, with several days of quite heavy flow one period and just a day or two of spotting the next. This can certainly be an annoyance, but it usually doesn't mean anything is wrong, and will usually correct itself within a few months. Sometimes, however, such an unpredictable pattern just continues indefinitely, or starts appearing sometime after a regular pattern of periods has been established, throwing everything off. In such cases, a visit to the family physician or other doctor may be in order.

Most often, irregular periods result from undetectable causes. Minor hormonal imbalances may sometimes, but not always, be at fault. Physical exhaustion or emotional stress at school or at home, very common in teenage years, may contribute. Poor eating habits, especially those that arise from bizarre or stringent crash diets aimed at fast weight loss, may also play a part. If the problem persists, the doctor may decide to prescribe certain hormones, particularly those found in oral birth control pills, to be taken for an interval of a few months. These hormones interfere temporarily with the ovulation cycle by blocking ovulation, and create a sort of "artificial menstrual period" at predetermined intervals according to how the medicine is taken. Such treatment isn't continued indefinitely, usually just long enough to get the menstrual periods established in a regular pattern. Regulated in this fashion, the periods usually remain regular when treatment is discontinued.

PAINFUL MENSTRUATION (CRAMPING)

The medical term for any kind of pain or discomfort associated with menstruation is **dysmenorrhea**, from Latin words meaning "difficult menstrual flow." In most cases, however, this refers to the rhythmic painful **cramping** in the lower abdomen, sometimes combined with aching in the small of the back or in the inner thighs, that begins just about when the period begins and may continue the length of the period.

Some girls get the idea, from talking to others, that practically everybody has painful menstrual cramps. This isn't quite the case—lots of women go through their entire lives without any serious discomfort. But many women—over 50 percent, according to some medical authorities—*do* experience *some* degree of discomfort, at least sometimes, during their periods, including mild headaches or backaches, and about 10 percent have such regular and severe trouble with cramps that they are seriously disabled for two or three days out of every period.

For years many doctors thought that women who complained of menstrual cramps were just nuisances. They thought the pain was all in the woman's head, and that since the cramping went away after a couple of days anyway, there was no need to fuss over it. But doctors don't take that attitude any longer. Today we know that most women who complain of menstrual cramps are suffering from real physical distress. Tiny hormonelike chemicals called **prostaglandins**, which are produced in the uterus as well as in other organs of the body, are now known to be at fault in many cases of menstrual cramping. No one is yet sure of the exact purpose of these prostaglandins, but we do know that one thing they do in the uterus is to cause uterine muscle fibers to contract. In many women these prostaglandins appear in extremely high concentrations shortly after ovulation has taken place. And studies have shown that those women who have frequent painful menstrual cramping have a much higher level of prostaglandins in their uterus at menstruation time than do women who have no cramps.

Nobody knows for sure why one woman will have a high level of prostaglandins and consequently suffer from menstrual cramps while another will have a low level and not be bothered at all. But a variety of medical treatments are available today to provide relief from this problem. For a girl who has nothing more than minor cramping for the first few hours after her period starts, a couple of aspirin tablets two or three times during the first day may be all that's needed. Because aspirin slightly reduces the blood's ability to clot, and thus might conceivably lead to heavier flow, some doctors recommend another mild pain-relieving medicine, *acetaminophen* (sold as Tylenol, Datril, etc.) as an alternative.

When such simple measures aren't enough, there are some bigger guns that can be used. If you have experienced painful cramping, or know someone else who has, you may also know that doctors will often prescribe a birth control pill to relieve the symptom. It is known that menstrual cramping occurs only in a cycle in which a woman has ovulated. The oral contraceptives (contraceptive meaning "to prevent pregnancy"), or birth control pills, supply a girl's body with estrogen and progesteronelike hormones that act in such a way to prevent ovulation and, therefore, cramps. The buildup of the inner lining of the uterus and the later loss of cells and blood in the menstrual period goes on much as usual, but the cramping is relieved.

This kind of medication, when properly used, is also a highly effective means of preventing pregnancy, since fertilization cannot occur without ovulation. However, birth control pills may sometimes have dangerous side effects on the body when used over a long period of time, and thus their use for any reason or for any extended period should be discussed carefully with the doctor.

For girls who can't take birth control pills, or don't want to, another totally different group of medicines can provide good relief for menstrual cramps. These are the so-called **antiprostaglandin** drugs which block the body's formation of prostaglandins and thus cut off the source of much menstrual cramping. Unlike birth control pills, which must be taken on a continuous schedule throughout the month, these medicines need be taken only for the two or three days when the cramping is occurring. One of these drugs, known as *ibuprofen* (trade names Advil or Nuprin), is even available over the counter in drugstores. But again, because of possible side effects, any of these drugs should be used only under a doctor's supervision.

In many women, menstrual cramping isn't related to anything else wrong with them—it just happens when menstruation time comes. But in some the cramping or other discomforts may be *secondary*—that is, they may arise from some other specific physical cause. In some cases, for instance, an infection of some sort in the reproductive organs may be at fault. Some women who use an **intrauterine device** (a plastic or metal device placed inside the uterus to prevent pregnancy) begin having menstrual cramps as soon as the device is put in place. Other women have an abnormal condition known as **endometriosis**, which leads to painful menstruation. (See page 50 for more about endometriosis.) Obviously, in such cases, it is necessary to identify and treat the underlying cause before the cramping can be effectively controlled. It is for this reason that any girl who has more than the most minor trouble with menstrual pain should see a doctor at least once for an examination and advice. There isn't any need to just "suffer in silence" these days.

MISSED PERIODS

The medical term for missed periods is **amenorrhea**, meaning, literally, "without menstrual flow." We have already described one kind of amenorrhea, when a girl's first menstrual period seems to be delayed far beyond the normal age. Another kind can occur when a young woman has been menstruating quite regularly for a period of time and then misses one or more periods.

Of course pregnancy is by far the most common cause for this second type of amenorrhea. We have seen that if a pregnancy occurs during an ovulation cycle, the expected menstrual period just doesn't occur. Neither does the next one, nor the next, on through the pregnancy. By the time a second period is missed, in such a case, other suggestive signs of pregnancy will also have begun to appear: fullness and tenderness of the breasts, for example, a sense of fullness in the lower abdomen, and often a tendency to feel nauseated in the mornings (morning sickness).

But pregnancy is not by any means the only reason for missing periods. Sometimes they are merely delayed, perhaps because of an illness, severe stress, or a drastic change in diet. Inadequate amounts of protein and iron, sometimes caused by adhering to a poorly planned vegetarian diet, can result not only in missed periods but also in severe **anemia**, a shortage of iron in the blood. Including beans, or eggs and milk, in a vegetarian diet can help prevent this from happening, and a return to a diet providing ample protein and iron will result in restoring normal periods.

A few women begin missing periods because they have developed a blockage of the cervix. A great many more, however, skip periods for no detectable reason at all. Often, in such cases, the doctor can provide treatment with hormones that artificially trigger the menstrual cycle. Once started, menstrual periods in most such cases resume their normal pattern.

Recently, however, doctors have identified two kinds of amenorrhea quite distinct from any we have mentioned above, and occurring far more commonly than anyone formerly realized. The first and most frequent of these is called **exercise amenorrhea**. It has been found that a great many girls and women who are seriously involved in athletics or strenuous daily exercise, such as distance running or jogging, gymnastics, ballet training, or competitive swimming, begin missing periods and, indeed, often don't ovulate while the exercise is going on. This is brought on, it is believed, by hormone changes that occur because of the strenuous exercise. It doesn't seem to do any particular harm, as far as is known, and seems to be completely reversible once the exercise is interrupted, but this can be one possible cause for missed periods among athletic or exercise-oriented girls.

Weight loss amenorrhea is a little more ominous. Lots of girls in their school years decide to go on crash diets in order to lose a lot of weight in a hurry, and sometimes these girls will stop menstruating. When this happens, the girl should recognize it as a clear sign that she is overdoing things, and should go back to normal eating patterns before she does her body serious harm.

Amenorrhea also appears as a major symptom in two less common but very dangerous weight-loss disorders known as **bulimia** (deliberately throwing up after eating to control weight) and **anorexia nervosa** (just not eating at all, to speak of). In these disorders, the missed periods are related not only to hormone imbalances but to real nutritional deficiencies as well, and serious, permanent injury to the body is possible. Prompt and expert medical help is needed to combat these problems.

EXCESSIVE MENSTRUAL FLOW

Within the range of normal that we have spoken of are light menstrual flows that last only a day or two and heavy flows that last five to seven days or more. In either case, the pattern is usually reasonably consistent from one period to the next. But some women, more often older women but occasionally girls, experience truly excessive, prolonged menstrual flows, a condition knowns as **menorrhagia**.

Such truly heavy bleeding episodes, especially when they are repeated, require a doctor's attention. They can be disabling, can drain a woman's body of its iron supply, and can cause anemia.

Sometimes heavy bleeding episodes are related to the loss of a pregnancy in its early stages (miscarriage). Other times, something may be out of order with the inner lining of the uterus—the woman may have developed benign, space-taking tumors called **fibroids** in the uterine wall, for example. In some cases it is necessary for the doctor to perform a surgical procedure called a **D&C** (for *dilatation and curettement*) in which the cervix or mouth of the uterus is dilated and a sample of tissue is scraped or curetted from the uterine lining under anesthesia in order to diagnose the reason for the excessive bleeding. But even when no cause is determined, even after a D&C, there are medications a doctor can prescribe to help control excessive flow. Anyone who experiences flow far in excess of her usual pattern should not hesitate to see a doctor.

PREMENSTRUAL
SYNDROME (PMS)

As we saw in chapter two, menstruation is a perfectly normal bodily function in sexually mature girls and women. It's a normal part of a woman's life, as natural and necessary as eating, drinking, or sleeping. But a certain number of women become aware of something distinctly *ab*normal that can happen to their bodies, and to the way they feel, during a period of a few days up to a week or more *before* their menstrual periods begin. This "something abnormal" often takes the form of a group of odd physical and emotional symptoms which doctors today call **premenstrual syndrome** or **PMS**, for want of any better name to call it.

The symptoms of PMS seem to involve both the body and the emotions in differing degrees in different women. Regarding bodily symptoms, a girl may find, a few days before her period is due, that she seems to feel bloated or puffy, headachy, or extra tired for no reason. Her breasts may become sore, and she may even notice a little puffiness or swelling of her ankles. She may also notice that she's unusually hungry for sweets or cookies or salty foods.

At the same time she may notice some rather mysterious emotional changes. She may feel restless, or depressed, or excessively irritable, snapping at her best friends for no reason—or she may just feel extremely nervous and tense, as if there were a coiled spring inside her just about ready to pop loose. She may have crying spells for no apparent reason, or just want to withdraw from other people. In extreme cases girls have told their doctors that they feel like they're going crazy for a few days, they just don't know *what* they're liable to do—and then their period starts and all the symptoms seem to disappear like magic.

What's going on here? Even the medical experts aren't sure, nor can they explain why the symptoms of PMS may vary so much from one woman to another, or seem so mild in some and so severe in others—but they *are* sure that magic doesn't have anything to do with it. Years ago many of these symptoms were written off as "psychological," but most doctors don't believe that anymore. It seems far more likely today that the symptoms of PMS, when they occur, are actually caused by a variety of chemical and hormonal changes that occur in the body during the days just before the period begins.

Exactly what these changes are is still not clear. Slight imbalances between estrogen and progesterone following ovulation may cause the body to retain excessive amounts of salt and water at this time, leading to a bloated, overstuffed feeling. Hormones may also cause soreness of the breasts to occur during this time, which could contribute even further to the emotional tension already present. Recent studies have shown that many women with severe premenstrual syndrome also have excessively high levels of other hormones in their bodies. Some doctors theorize that once the menstrual period begins, the offending hormone levels tend to drop off sharply and the kidneys begin releasing retained salt and water, thus accounting for the sudden disappearance of symptoms.

Whatever exactly is going on (and a great deal of research today is devoted to finding out what), PMS does seem to affect a great many girls and women to some degree or another. One medical authority estimates that some 30 to 40 percent of women have some degree of PMS, and perhaps 5 percent find their lives severely disrupted by it. For most girls with mild symptoms that only last a few days, doctors today recommend a common sense approach: monitoring the diet to reduce sweets and salty foods during the premenstrual interval; getting plenty of sleep and exercise; reducing the pressures of a busy schedule as much as possible during those "target days"; and attempting to avoid upsetting situations or people.

For those with more severe or disrupting symptoms, a visit to the doctor can be helpful. When there is actual retention of fluid, for example, the doctor may prescribe a *diuretic*—a medicine that forces the kidneys to pass extra salt and water in the urine—starting a week or so before the period. In other cases, medications may be prescribed to lower the levels of various hormones. For the most part, when symptoms are severe enough to require medical treatment, the particular treatment will be targeted at the woman's individual symptoms. And even though PMS is not yet clearly understood, it is not something that anyone has to "just live with." Treatment can indeed help.

ENDOMETRIOSIS

Most of the problems of menstruation we've been talking about—things like temporary amenorrhea or premenstrual syndrome—sit on the borderline between normal and abnormal. In minor cases they are within the range of normal, but in severe cases they're abnormal and need medical attention. But another disorder, known as **endometriosis**, is a different matter. This is an extremely painful condition which is *never* normal. What is more, it does not tend to go away by itself, can be quite disabling, and is very difficult to treat successfully.

The name comes from *endometrium*, the medical term for the inner lining of the uterus. In most women the menstrual material always flows down and out. But in certain women, for unknown reasons, a small amount of menstrual flow containing cells from the uterine lining tends to back up, moving *up* the Fallopian tube and escaping out into the lower abdominal

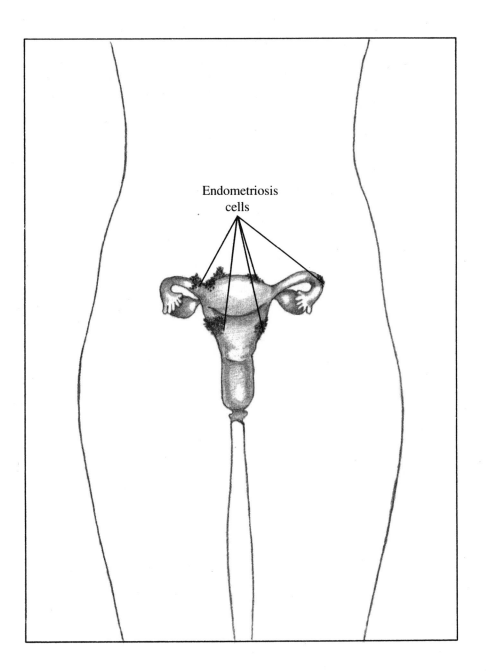
Endometriosis
cells

cavity outside the uterus. Here clusters of these endometrial cells may become attached to the pelvic region, to the back of the uterus, to the outside of the tubes, or to the ovaries. The cells then begin to grow on their own, forming little islands of endometrial tissue.

No one knows why this happens in one woman and not in another. Some experts claim it happens more frequently in the woman whose uterus is tilted slightly back rather than forward. Whatever the cause, once these little islands of endometrial tissue have formed outside the uterus, they respond to hormones exactly as if they were still inside. Thus, before ovulation, these clusters of cells begin to grow and enlarge just as the lining of the uterus does. But because of their position, they cause pain, and the larger they get, the more painful they become. Not until menstruation itself occurs, with the uterine lining breaking down and being discharged as menstrual flow, do these islands of endometrial cells begin to shrink so that the pain subsides.

Women with endometriosis often suffer pain in the lower abdomen recurrently month after month. Pregnancy relieves the pain, since there are no ovulation cycles during pregnancy, but these women—for reasons unknown—often have a great deal of difficulty becoming pregnant. The condition can be treated, but not always too successfully. In some cases, treatment with hormone combinations, including birth control pills, can relieve the pain substantially. In other more stubborn cases a lighted instrument known as a **laparoscope** can be inserted, under anesthesia, into the lower abdomen on a "search and destroy mission" to find the endometrial implants and remove them surgically. So far, however, no completely successful way has been found to cure this condition.

MANAGING YOUR MENSTRUATION

The beginning of menstruation means an obvious change in your life. Thus, even before your menarche, you should be aware of the simple, modern ways to take proper care of your mentrual flow and of the methods available to relieve any discomfort you experience. You should also know what physical activities you can continue during your period and what you might want to avoid. And finally, if any serious menstrual problems do arise, you need to know what doctor to consult and what kinds of examinations he or she will be likely to perform.

PADS AND TAMPONS

Believe it or not, there was no such thing as a disposable pad before World War I, just seventy-odd years ago. Tampons for internal use are even newer. According to one account, it was an acute wartime shortage of cotton cloth (used for battle dressings) that led to the invention of the cottony fluff now used in disposable pads.

Most girls, when they start their periods, use **sanitary napkins**—narrow, oblong pads of soft, absorbent stuff wrapped in a porous outer lining—to absorb the flow. Napkins are designed to be worn externally, fitting snugly between the legs. Some are kept in place by a narrow, elastic belt worn around the waist next to the skin and attached to the napkin front and back. But most napkins now have an adhesive strip on the outer surface that effectively attaches the napkin to the panties, thus making a belt unnecessary. To meet individual needs, napkins may also contain differing amounts of absorbent material—an extra amount for heavy flow, a smaller amount for mid-period, and so forth.

Napkins should be changed before they become full, an average of four or more times a day during heavy flow, perhaps two or three changes daily toward the end of a period. When removed they should be placed in disposable bags or wrapped in toilet paper and discarded in the trash or garbage. *Never* flush sanitary napkins down the toilet; they will plug up a plumbing system in no time flat.

Although they are handy, inexpensive, tidy, and designed to be form fitting, napkins do have some disadvantages. They can be bulky and awkward for girls who are physically active; they can't be worn while swimming or bathing; and disposing of them can be a nuisance. **Tampons** were invented to get around these problems. A tampon is nothing more than a small cylinder of expandable, absorbent material designed to be inserted into the vagina during a menstrual period. Once in the vaginal canal, the tampon expands and absorbs the menstrual flow internally. The tampon comes with a good length of string attached, part of which remains outside the vagina so the tampon can be pulled out when it is full.

Tampons, like napkins, come in various sizes. They are usually easy to insert. Some brands have no applicator. Others come packed inside narrow cardboard or plastic insertion tubes. All you need to do is to insert one end of the tampon or tube into the vaginal opening, make sure it is pointed in the right direction and that the string is left to hang free on the outside, and push in on the tampon or inserter end of the tube. Any applicator may then be discarded; the tampon will be placed within the vagina where it belongs.

To get the insertion tube or tampon to enter the body in the right direction—that is, in the same direction as the vaginal canal—you will need at least one of your hips flexed. You can accomplish this by sitting on the toilet seat, spreading your legs, and pointing the tampon or insertion tube at an upward angle toward the small of your back. Or, you can stand with one foot on a chair, or with both legs spread and your knees slightly bent while inserting the tampon. Lubrication isn't usually necessary, but it's perfectly okay to use a little cold cream or lubricating jelly to help while you are learning. To remove the tampon, simply pull gently but firmly on the string. Should the string break or otherwise become unusable (this can happen, but only rarely), don't panic. Your fingers will easily be able to reach the tampon and remove it.

Many girls have heard they could lose their virginity (that is, break the hymen) by using tampons. This is *very* unlikely to happen. The tampon inserter tip is barely ⅝ inch (1.6 cm) in diameter. Most girls have quite enough space at the vaginal opening to insert this tip right past the hymen with no difficulty. You would have to be extremely rough with yourself to injure this bit of tissue, and, if you were, discomfort would stop you before you did any harm. A few girls really *don't* have the necessary space or can't quite manage to get tampons inserted; these girls should stick with napkins until a doctor can help them.

Tampons (as well as *cardboard* insertion tubes) may be

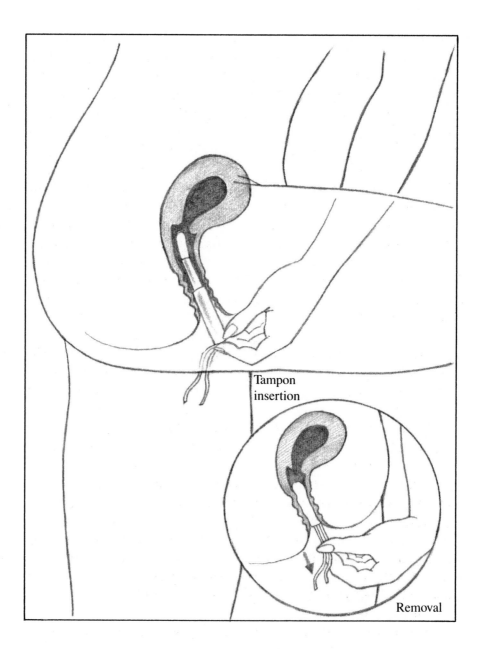

Tampon
insertion

Removal

flushed down the toilet. They should be changed at least every four to six hours whether they are full or not—and remember to remove the last one when your period is ended. Never use more than one tampon at a time. If one is not sufficient protection, try using a combination of napkins and tampons, or just napkins alone, until the flow has lightened.

TOXIC SHOCK SYNDROME (TSS)

Handy and convenient as tampons may be, there is one serious health problem that anyone using tampons should know about: a disease known as **toxic shock syndrome** or **TSS**, which can occur in women using tampons during their menstrual periods.

TSS was first identified in 1979 when five previously healthy young women in Minnesota became extremely ill during a menstrual period, with sudden fever, vomiting and diarrhea, a sunburnlike skin rash and sagging blood pressure. During 1980 and 1981, hundreds of similar cases were reported, most of them in menstruating women, and about 10 percent of those early victims died.

Most of the TSS victims were using tampons when the disease struck, and upon careful investigation, it was found that many of them were using a new type of "superabsorbent" tampon that had recently appeared on the market. As soon as these "*super tampons*" were withdrawn from sale by their manufacturers, the number of new cases of TSS reported dropped very sharply.

New cases still do occasionally appear, however, and most of these cases in menstruating women seem to be related to tampon use. Today we know that TSS is caused by bacteria—

specifically, by a certain variety of Staphylococcus organism. This germ, which is all around us, commonly lives on the surface of our skin. It also lives in the vaginas of about 10 percent of all menstruating women, and in most cases does no harm at all. But under certain special circumstances, especially when the outflow of menstrual fluid is too completely obstructed by a tampon (or by such birth control devices as diaphragms or contraceptive sponges), the Staphylococcus organism can begin producing a deadly poison or **toxin**, which can be absorbed into the body and spread through the bloodstream. It is this toxin that causes the dangerous shocklike symptoms and other signs of TSS.

If all this makes the use of tampons sound pretty grim, there's a brighter side to the picture. The principle offenders— "superabsorbent" tampons—have been removed from the market, and millions of women still use regular tampons to control their menstrual flow every month without any problem whatever. Recent research suggests that only about 5 percent of the population may be vulnerable to toxic shock at all—but there's no easy way for you to find out whether you are one of them or not. What you *can* do, if you choose to use tampons, is follow some simple rules recommended by doctors who know the most about TSS:

Read—and be sure you understand—the printed TSS warning that comes with every package of tampons. It's required to be there by the Food and Drug Administration, for your protection.

Use the least absorbent tampons that will control your flow.

If possible, alternate tampons with sanitary napkins or pads during your periods.

Change tampons at least three to four times daily, whether you need to or not.

Most important of all, **be alert for the warning signs of toxic shock syndrome listed below:**

- **sudden fever of 102°F (38.9°C) or more**
- **nausea and vomiting, or diarrhea**
- **a sunburnlike red rash on the palms of the hands or elsewhere on the body**
- **dizziness or faintness upon standing up suddenly** (a sign of low or sagging blood pressure)
- **a sore throat, or red, irritated eyes**
- **severe muscle aching**

If you develop symptoms like these during your period, remove the tampon at once if you're using one, and contact a doctor. Fortunately, with prompt diagnosis and appropriate treatment, the few people today who *do* develop TSS usually recover quickly and completely.

LIVING THROUGH YOUR PERIOD

There are only a few things you really should avoid just because of a menstrual period. Fifty years ago menstruating girls were faced with a list of do's and don'ts a mile long—mostly don'ts. Today it's mostly do's.

Bathing. Regular bathing, grooming, and shampooing will help you look and feel your best always, and period time is no time to break your routine. If you are using napkins, showers are easiest and cleanest, although tub baths are okay toward the end of a period. Remove your pad before your bath, of course, and replace it with a fresh pad afterward. Water temperature isn't important as long as it isn't scalding hot or shockingly cold. Tub baths or showers are fine throughout your period if you have a tampon in place. But change your tampon after a shower or bath.

Swimming. With tampons you can swim or surf anytime without any problem. But if you wear napkins, for reasons of public hygiene you should avoid swimming altogether during a heavy flow, and stay out of pools, hot tubs, and other public bathing areas until your period is over. (Lake or ocean swimming is fine for light days.)

Other sports and activities. Girls no longer have to be wall-flowers during their periods. Even the most active sports will do you no harm as long as you feel like doing them. In fact, girls who are physically active all month long are less likely to have trouble with menstrual cramps than girls who sit around like lumps all the time. Even as little as a half hour of brisk walking every day can pay off in more comfortable periods. However, don't exhaust yourself, and get plenty of sleep at night. (These last do's and don'ts apply whether you are menstruating or not.)

Diet. Ordinarily there are no particularly good or bad foods for menstruation—no special items you should or shouldn't eat. A balanced diet of nutritious food is good for you any time of the month. (If you have trouble with the symptoms of premenstrual syndrome that we mentioned on page 48, it may be helpful to reduce your intake of sweets and salty foods during the premenstrual interval.) You should, however, try to drink a little more fluid than normal during your periods—eight to ten glasses of water, fruit juice, or milk a day. This will help prevent constipation, a condition that can sometimes contribute to the severity of cramps.

Social activities. Why not? School activities, basketball games, parties, dances—all of the activities you would normally take part in are perfectly fine during menstrual periods, as long as you feel like doing them.

RELIEVING CRAMPS
AND OTHER DISCOMFORTS

As we saw earlier, many girls do have cramps or headaches during their periods. Some girls have them just occasionally; others have them quite regularly. Often these problems are minor and are easily manageable by the girl herself without any professional help. Here are a few tips:

Keeping in shape. Regular, moderate exercise all month long, just keeping your body in reasonable trim, will help prevent cramps and will reduce their severity when they do occur. Take plenty of fluids to keep bowel movements regular.

Medicines. In many cases the discomfort of cramps can be reduced by taking one of the simple over-the-counter pain-relieving medicines such as aspirin or acetaminophen (Tylenol). Almost all the special medicines you see advertised for menstrual distress really contain one of those two drugs as their major ingredient. In addition, an over-the-counter (that is, available without prescription) form of one of the antiprostaglandin drugs, ibuprofen, sold under such trade names as Advil or Nuprin, has become available. Used two or three times a day according to directions on the bottle, any of these medicines will usually help relieve cramps and headaches as well. (*Never take any stronger pain medicine without specific directions from your doctor.*)

Physical and mental measures. Sometimes a heating pad or hot-water bottle on the abdomen will help relieve cramps. If you use a hot-water bottle, use hot tap water, not boiling water, and wrap the bottle in a towel or T-shirt to keep from burning yourself.

Some people claim that "mind over matter" can help, too. If you practice meditation or yoga, try using it to counteract cramps and headaches. In recent years biofeedback techniques have also been used for both menstrual cramps and headaches, with a certain amount of success—but these techniques really require expert professional guidance and lots of hard work to make them effective.

Exercises. A thousand different exercises have been recommended for cramps, which should give you a clue that no one of them is consistently helpful. Some, however, may be worth trying. Shoulder stands, for instance, may redistribute or release painful gas bubbles in the intestine and help relieve cramping. Other frequently used exercises include abdominal pumping (back flat, knees bent; push abdomen out during deep beathing, then pull it in sharply as you let the breath out), twisting exercises (back flat, arms out; lift one leg and reach over to touch the floor on the other side with your foot, then back and repeat with the other leg), and the side arc (stand erect, side to the wall about 16 inches [40 cm] away; push hips over to touch the wall, then return to erect position and repeat). Such exercises increase circulation to the pelvis and thus may help to relieve cramps.

THE DOCTOR
IN THE PICTURE

Nobody really *likes* to go to a doctor, but if you are having real and serious menstrual problems—severe and recurrent cramps and pain, for instance, missed periods, or repeated excessive flow—then it's wise to seek professional help.

Shoulder stand

Abdominal pumping

Twisting exercise

Side arc

Three kinds of doctors have experience dealing with menstrual problems. The first is the **family practice physician.** He or she encounters such problems frequently, and either knows how to treat them or knows what specialist to direct you to. Perhaps more experienced is the specialist in **obstetrics and gynecology,** or OB-GYN doctor for short. Obstetrics is concerned with the care of pregnancies; gynecology refers to the diagnosis and treatment of disorders of the female reproductive organs. Finally, a fairly new kind of doctor is the modern specialist in **adolescent medicine.**

Today there are many woman doctors in all three of these fields; girls who prefer not to have a male doctor examine them would do well to choose one of these. The most important consideration in choosing a doctor, however, aside from professional capabilities, is that you feel relaxed and comfortable with the person.

Any doctor you see about menstrual problems will probably need to perform a **pelvic examination,** sometimes called an "internal." No matter what you may have heard, the pelvic exam need not be a particularly painful or distressing experience.

The patient, in a loose gown, lies as relaxed as possible on her back on an examining table with knees bent and legs spread. First the doctor makes a brief examination of the external organs, looking for abnormal structures, signs of external infection, rashes, or anything else out of order. Next is the vaginal exam, which requires a narrow instrument shaped like a duckbill and known as a **speculum** (from the Latin word meaning "to look") to be inserted into the vagina. The instrument is warmed and lubricated before use. A special extra-narrow speculum may be used when the patient has never had sexual relations, in order not to disturb the hymen. When the

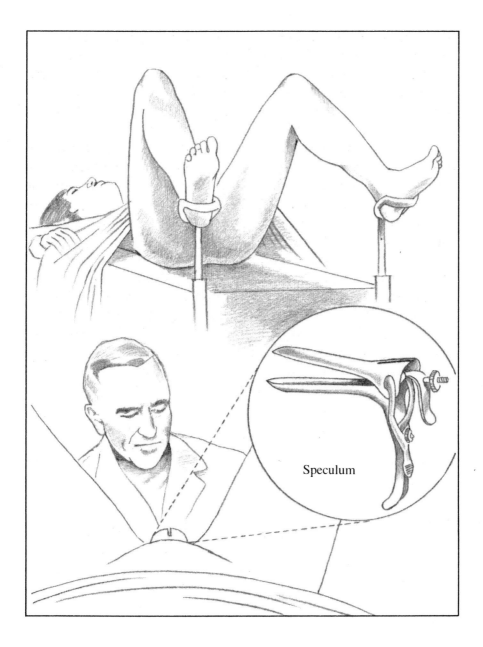

Speculum

two paddles of the duckbill are separated slightly, the doctor can see the cervix as well as the inside walls of the vagina. At this time the doctor will often take a **Pap smear** (a few cells taken from the cervix and vagina) for cancer examination and, if indicated, a sample of any vaginal discharge to examine for possible bacterial, yeast, or fungus infection.

This vaginal examination takes about a minute and is usually quite painless. Then, with the speculum withdrawn, an internal or bimanual ("two-handed") exam is done to examine the internal reproductive organs. The doctor usually stands at the patient's side with one hand on the patient's lower abdomen. With the other hand in a sterile surgical glove, the doctor inserts one or two fingers into the vagina until the finger meets the patient's cervix. By gently pressing the abdomen, the doctor can then actually feel the size, shape, and normality of the patient's uterus, ovaries, and Fallopian tubes between his or her fingers. As a final step, the doctor may insert a finger of the gloved hand into the rectum to feel for abnormalities—often a good way to detect endometriosis, for example.

In addition to a pelvic exam, the doctor will carefully check the patient's heart and lungs and the thyroid gland in the front of the neck. The breasts and abdomen will be examined for abnormalities as well. Finally, certain simple lab tests—a blood count, for example, and a urine analysis—will be done. If necessary, more complex lab tests of the blood and urine may be undertaken, depending on the problem and the findings of the preliminary physical exam.

You will certainly not want to seek out a doctor about every minor twinge that may arise during menstruation. But when real and distressing problems turn up, doctors can offer a great deal of help.

MENSTRUATION IN YOUR LIFE

From the very beginning we have emphasized that menstruation is a normal, healthy bodily function. But of course it is far more than that. For each and every one of you, the way you feel about your menstruation, and, in fact, about your entire emerging sexuality, will deeply affect your emotional growth and development, your self-image (the picture of yourself that you carry around in your head), your sense of self-esteem (the way you feel about yourself inside), and a dozen other aspects of your life. It will even inevitably affect the way other people regard you.

To get some background on how girls generally feel about menstruation, I spent several evenings at a small college in the Pacific Northwest, talking to a group of a half-dozen college girls. These girls were all between eighteen and twenty years old. They had come from various parts of the country and even from abroad—one girl's home was in Hong Kong. All of them clearly remembered how it was when they had begun menstruating, and all were willing to answer my questions and describe how they felt about different things at the time. Here are just a few of the things they said. (The names, of course, have been changed to protect the girls' privacy.)

Q: I've heard it said that many girls find the beginning of menstruation a very distressing and alarming time of life. Were any of you frightened or worried or especially upset at that time?

Sara: Frightened? Not really. I think I felt more of a sense of relief than anything else. From the time I was eleven I kept thinking, "Well, it's going to happen any time now," and then it didn't, and this got to be a drag after a while. And then all of a sudden, there it was, and I sort of thought, "Well, thank God I can quit worrying about it now!"

Liu Tang: I think my mother *tried* to scare me, a little. She kept telling me how I was going to have to be very suspicious and careful about boys now, and things like that. But *I* wasn't scared. I wasn't even much interested in boys, at least not for a couple more years.

Q: How did the rest of you feel about boys? Did menstruation make any changes in that?

Sharon: Just that all of them seemed so *young* all of a sudden. Here most of them were still going around with their voices squeaking and busily admiring two hairs on their chins, while I was sprouting out all over. I felt *much* older and more mature. Of course I wasn't, but that's the way I felt.

Mary: I had the feeling that boys were becoming much more wary of *me*. Just a little while before I'd been a real tomboy. I was a better baseball player than any of them, and I could outswear them all and even slug it out with them if I had to—but then all of a sudden everything changed and we couldn't be pals anymore. They got very nervous and self-conscious and wanted to hold hands all the time instead of playing baseball. But then, I was a little nervous and self-conscious, too. It was like we both had a whole new set of equations to try to figure out and get in balance. Guys had to figure out where they fit into those equations, and so did I.

Q: Did you spend a lot of time thinking about this?
Mary: Oh, not much. [Laughing] Just constantly.
Marge: I don't think I thought about it that much. After all, we were still kids, just trying our best to figure out how to be adult human beings.

Q: What do you think the boys thought about menstruation?
Marge: Well, most of them seemed to know all about it, or let on that they did. Mostly, I think that they knew something had happened, but most of them weren't quite sure what.
Bev: I remember I was just terribly worried about what the boys thought. Some of the older girls kept telling us how the boys would all avoid you when you were having your period, and how they could tell you were menstruating by looking in your eyes. I even wore dark glasses for a while—talk about a dead giveaway! Of course in a year or so we knew that was all a lot of nonsense.
Sara: I heard those things, too, but they didn't bother me. But then I was pretty bashful in those days. I had a lot of acne and thought I was just grotesquely ugly, so I pretended I didn't *care* what the boys thought.

Q: Earlier one or two of you spoke of your periods with a certain amount of annoyance or even anger. I think it was Liu Tang who said they were a "big fat bother." Do any of you actually *enjoy* anything about having periods? Do you think there's anything good about them? Do they provide any sort of advantage?

Mary: Oh, yes! There's no question about it. It's hard to put it into words, but I think there's a certain comfortable feeling of *rightness* about things when your period comes. It's as if your body is sending you nice loud signals that you're in good shape and everything is working the way it should. You're a whole, complete person.

Sharon: It does give you a sense that things are all right, maybe a sense of maturity, too.

Q: One last question: I've heard people say that menstruation makes a girl a woman. What do you think about that?

Mary: [Long pause] Well, now wait a minute. That certainly doesn't sound right to *me*. Haven't you got it backwards?

Sara: You might say that *ovulating* makes a girl a woman because then she can get pregnant—but does just being able to get pregnant make a girl a woman? I don't think menstruation makes you *anything* in particular.

Marge: I'm not sure that getting pregnant necessarily makes you a woman either. What about the thirteen- and four-teen-year-old girls who get pregnant? I don't think they're *women*, pregnant or not. They're just teenage girls who've gotten pregnant.

But all the girls agreed that Sharon gave the best answer of all:

Sharon: Of course menstruating, all by itself, doesn't make you a woman. It couldn't. Really, menstruation is just telling you that your body has become sexually mature enough so that you're capable of having a baby. That's *part* of being a woman, and a very important part, too, but that isn't all there is to it. It seems to me that menstruation is just one of a whole flock of signals a girl gets in her early teens that tells her she's beginning to develop into a mature woman and she'd better start getting ready for it. Menstruation tells you *things are changing—better pay attention.* But really, becoming a mature woman involves a million other things, too—learning how to be responsible for what you do, learning to make your word good so that other people can always count on it, developing good judgment and learning how to use it, learning how to develop really mature, responsible relationships with men—a million other things enter into the picture.

A million other things indeed. If nothing else, we have seen how many different patterns menstruation alone can take. No one can say to you, "This is what is going to happen to you when you begin menstruating." There is too much variation from one person to the next, all within the range of normal. Menstruation is an *individual* matter, and it is just one part of a grand pattern of physical and emotional events that occurs as you leave your childhood behind and steadily develop into an adult.

GLOSSARY OF IMPORTANT TERMS

(*Note:* Specific organs of the male and female body are not included in this glossary. Definitions and illustrations of them may be found by referring to the index.)

Acne: Pimples; a skin disorder related to androgens in the body.

Adolescent medicine: A medical specialty dealing with diseases and other medical problems of teenaged young people.

Amenorrhea: Medical term for missed periods.

Analgesic: Any pain-relieving medicine.

Androgens: The male sex hormones produced mainly in the testes and the cortex of the adrenal gland.

Anemia: A shortage of iron in the blood.

Anorexia nervosa: A dangerous physical and emotional disorder in which a person, obsessed with remaining slender, either cannot or will not eat normally and may ultimately starve to death.

Anti-prostaglandin: A drug which blocks the formation of special hormones known as prostaglandins which, among other things, can cause menstrual cramping.

Bulimia: An eating disorder, similar to anorexia nervosa (see above), in which a person, obsessed with remaining slender but craving food, will periodically eat excessively and then deliberately vomit to avoid putting on weight.

Cramping: Discomfort or pain sometimes felt in the lower abdomen during menstrual periods. Caused by contractions of muscle fibers in the uterus.

Cyst: A collection of fluid; if formed on any ovary, it may throw a period off.

D&C: Dilation and curettement of the uterus—an operation in which the uterine canal is dilated and cells are scraped from inside the uterus, often done to diagnose or treat abnormal uterine bleeding.

Dysmenorrhea: The medical term for any period discomfort, but usually refers to cramping.

Embryo: A baby in its early developing stages. The embryo usually lodges and grows inside the uterus.

Endometriosis: A serious, painful disorder related to a disturbance in the menstrual flow.

Estrogens: Female sex hormones produced mainly in the ovaries.

Exercise amenorrhea: Delayed menstruation or missed periods resulting from vigorous daily physical exercise.

Family practice physician: A doctor with special professional certification for treating illnesses of all members of the family. Many "family doctors" or "general practitioners" today are certified as family practice specialists.

Female reproductive cycle: The entire cycle, controlled by hormones, during which the female becomes prepared for pregnancy.

Fertilization: The penetration of a ripe ovum by a sperm cell. The two cells fuse together and then develop into an embryo.

Fibroids: Noncancerous growths of fibrous and muscular tissue that sometimes develop in the uterine wall and may contribute to excessive menstrual flow.

Follicle-stimulating hormone (FSH): A hormone from the pituitary gland that helps stimulate the ripening of an ovum in a woman's ovary.

Germ cells: The special sex cells—mature ova from the female, sperm cells from the male—which fuse together following sexual intercourse to cause a pregnancy.

Growth spurt: The increase in body growth that occurs at the time of sexual maturation, usually between ages eleven and fourteen.

Hormones: Chemical substances formed in certain glands and organs of the body and carried by the bloodstream to affect the behavior of other organs.

Imperforate hymen: A rare malformation of the tissue that normally covers part of the opening to the vagina in females who have not yet had sexual relations.

Intrauterine device: A small birth-control device made of metal or plastic inserted into the woman's uterus to prevent pregnancy.

Lactogenic hormone: The hormone that works with estrogens to enlarge a woman's breasts and enable them to produce milk.

Laparoscope: A narrow, lighted tube that can be inserted through a tiny opening in the abdominal wall to examine the organs within the abdomen or pelvis.

Luteinizing hormone (LH): The hormone used to help form the corpus luteum tissue in the ovary during ovulation.

Menarche: A girl's first menstrual period.

Menopause: The time of life, usually around age fifty, when a woman no longer produces reproductive cells and ceases to have menstrual periods.

Menorrhagia: An excessive, prolonged menstrual flow.

Menses: The cellular material and blood that passes out of the body during a menstrual period. More commonly known as the menstrual flow.

Menstruation: The shedding of cells from the uterine lining, together with some blood, which occurs when a female egg cell has not been fertilized.

Mittelschmerz: Twinges of discomfort in the lower abdomen occasionally felt by some women during ovulation.

Obstetrics and gynecology (OB-GYN): The medical specialty that specializes in the treatment of female reproductive organs and pregnancy.

Ovulation: The release of a ripened ovum from the ovary where it was formed. Upon release it travels down the Fallopian tube toward the uterus.

Ovum (pl. Ova): A female reproductive cell, the egg cell.

Pap smear: A scraping of cells from the vagina and cervix, used to determine if cancer is present.

Pelvic examination: The usual examination doctors perform to check for diseases or abnormalities of the female reproductive organs.

Period: The menstrual period, that is, the interval of days approximately every four weeks when menstruation takes place.

Placenta: The special organ that grows within the uterus during pregnancy to help the body supply oxygen and nutrients to a growing baby.

Premenstrual syndrome (PMS): The emotional and physical changes often experienced just prior to or at the beginning of menstrual periods. Premenstrual syndrome is caused by hormones in the body.

Progesterone: A female sex hormone that helps support the ovum until it is fertilized and protects the growth of the new baby if pregnancy occurs.

Prolactin: Another name for lactogenic hormone.

Prostaglandins: Hormones manufactured in the uterus (among other places) that sometimes produce menstrual cramping.

Puberty: The time of sexual maturation; that is, the time when both males and females become physically able to reproduce.

Sanitary napkins: Narrow, oblong pads of absorbent cottony material used to absorb menstrual flow externally.

Secondary sex characteristics: Those bodily manifestations of sex not directly related to reproduction but which essentially prepare the body for it.

Speculum: A tubular instrument a doctor can insert into the vagina to permit examination of the cervix (the lower end of the uterus).

Sperm: A male reproductive cell. Has a long, whiplike tail.

Tampon: A narrow, compressed cylinder of absorbent material designed to be inserted into the vagina to absorb menstrual flow internally.

Toxic shock syndrome (TSS): A group of symptoms, including fever, skin rash, and collapse, caused by poisons produced by certain staph bacteria growing in the vagina or elsewhere and recently found to be related to the use of "super absorbent" tampons.

Toxins: Poisons produced by various bacteria that can be absorbed into the bloodstream and damage organs or tissues.

Tumor: An overgrowth of cells which, if it forms on an ovary, can throw off a period.

Weight loss amenorrhea: Delayed menstruation or missed periods sometimes accompanying sudden, marked weight loss.

INDEX

ABOUT THE AUTHOR

Alan E. Nourse is a former practicing physician and a distinguished science writer for children and adults. For Franklin Watts, he has authored many popular First Books in the health area, including *Viruses* and *Your Immune System.*

In 1983, he was the recipient of the American Academy of Family Physicians Journalism Award for outstanding journalism in writing on family medicine and health care.

Dr. Nourse lives with his wife, Ann, in Thorp, Washington. They have four grown children.

612.662 Nourse, Alan E.
Nourse   Menstruation

c.2

$9.90

DATE			
JE -3 '92			